# LET'S EXPLORE LIFE SCIENCE

## Exploring
# HEREDITY

**Ella Hawley**

**PowerKiDS** press™

New York

Published in 2013 by The Rosen Publishing Group, Inc.
29 East 21st Street, New York, NY 10010

First Edition

Editor: Jennifer Way
Book Design: Kate Laczynski

Photo Credits: Cover, pp. 4–5, 6, 7, 9, 10, 11, 12–13, 15, 16 (left, right), 20 Shutterstock. com; cover (kitten) PhotoDisc; cover (rose) iStockphoto/Thinkstock; p. 8 Hemera/Thinkstock; p. 12 Pasieka/Getty Images; p. 14 Hulton Archive/Getty Images; p. 18 Maciej Frolow/Getty Images; p. 19 Don Mason/Getty Images; p. 21 (right) Dr. Stanley Flegler/Getty Images; p. 21 (left) © www.iStockphoto.com/Anthony Enns; p. 22 Peter Dazeley/Getty Images.

Library of Congress Cataloging-in-Publication Data

Hawley, Ella.
 Exploring heredity / by Ella Hawley. — 1st ed.
    p. cm. — (Let's explore life science)
 Includes index.
 ISBN 978-1-4488-6174-3 (library binding) — ISBN 978-1-4488-6312-9 (pbk.) — ISBN 978-1-4488-6313-6 (6-pack)
 1. Heredity, Human—Juvenile literature. 2. Genes—Juvenile literature. I. Title.
 QH431.H352 2013
 599.93'5—dc23
                                                    2011023999

Manufactured in the United States of America

CPSIA Compliance Information: Batch #316260PK: For Further Information contact Rosen Publishing, New York, New York at 1-800-237-9932

# CONTENTS

# What Is Heredity?

Has anyone ever told you that you have your mother's smile or the same curly hair your grandfather had? Members of families often **resemble** each other. We share **traits** with our parents and our brothers and sisters. This is because many traits are passed down from parents to their children. The passing down of these traits is called **heredity**.

You might wonder how traits can be passed on to another person. The data that makes us look, act, or sound a certain way is held in tiny **genes**. Genes are parts of the **cells** in our bodies.

Parent pass down traits to their children. This is why there is often a strong resemblance among siblings or between family members.

# It's in the Genes

Genes have an important job. They are the building blocks that make every living thing what it is. There are genes that have the data for making your skin, your heart, your hair, and every other part of you. They have the code that makes your cells take on different jobs. They also have the code that makes you resemble your family but also makes you unique.

There are about 25,000 genes in the human body. The genes make **proteins**. Proteins are like little machines in our cells that make our bodies work as they should. Every cell has thousands of proteins, all of which are built by genes.

Every living thing has its own genetic code. Scientists have mapped the genetic code of animals such as horses (below) and dogs (left). This helps scientists better understand how genes work.

# Mixing It Up

Each kitten in this litter has the same parents. The parents' genes combined in different ways so that each kitten has a one-of-a-kind mix of its parents' traits.

You likely do not look exactly the same as other people in your family. This is because you have copies of genes from both parents, not just one. The genes you have been given from each parent combine. The ways in which genes are expressed, or show up in offspring, are traits. Hair color and eye color are traits. Every time your parents have a baby, they pass down a whole new combination of their genes. Some traits may match yours, but others may not. Each living thing is one of a kind!

Identical twins have the exact same genetic makeup, while fraternal, or nonidentical, twins do not.

# The Right Ingredients

Roses come in many different colors. Most roses you see were made by crossing different types of roses to get a certain color.

An octopus is an octopus because of the ingredients that make up its cells. A rose is a rose instead of a peach tree for the same reason. The genetic recipe that makes a plant or animal begins when these organisms **reproduce**. Each parent organism gives half of the ingredients for the recipe.

This is why you might have some traits from your mother and some from your father.

Plants and animals from different **species** cannot reproduce. It would be like trying to mix two different recipes. It just does not work!

This boy gets his red hair from his mother. It is a trait that she passed to him.

# Chromosomes

This is a chromosome. Chromosomes carry genetic information.

In human reproduction, a **sperm** cell from the male joins with an egg cell from a female. Each of these cells has 23 **chromosomes**. Chromosomes contain genes and other important data. When these cells join, they make a new cell that has 46 chromosomes. These cells split, making copies of all the chromosomes.

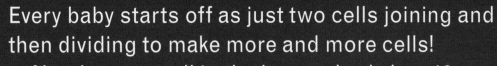

Every baby starts off as just two cells joining and then dividing to make more and more cells!

Nearly every cell in the human body has 46 chromosomes. The genes in the chromosomes tell these cells what kind of cell they will be. The chromosomes and genes are inside the nucleus, or center, of each cell.

By the time a baby is born, it has developed from just two cells to be made up of many millions of cells!

# Mendel and the Peas

People have been trying to understand how heredity works for a long time. In the 1800s, an Austrian monk named Gregor Mendel made some important discoveries. Many people call Mendel the father of genetics for his findings.

Mendel studied pea plants and their offspring. He crossed a pea plant with green pods with one that had yellow pods. You might

Gregor Mendel lived from 1822 until 1884.

14

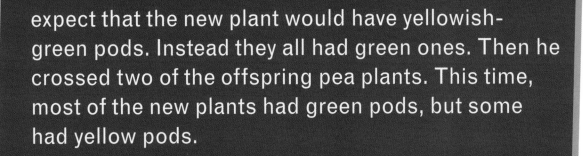

expect that the new plant would have yellowish-green pods. Instead they all had green ones. Then he crossed two of the offspring pea plants. This time, most of the new plants had green pods, but some had yellow pods.

Mendel chose to work with pea plants because they were easy to grow and it was easy to control the crossing of the plants.

# Which Gene Is the Boss?

Mendel's findings showed him that the genes for pea-pod color came in pairs. It also showed him that the green-pod gene was the **dominant** one in the pair. If the pea plant had two genes for green pea pods, then the pods were green. The same thing happened if it had one green gene and one yellow gene. The yellow gene was there, but it was weaker, or **recessive**. This means it took a back seat to the dominant gene.

Some plants had two yellow-pod genes, though. These ones were the few plants that had yellow pods when the green and yellow parent plants were crossed.

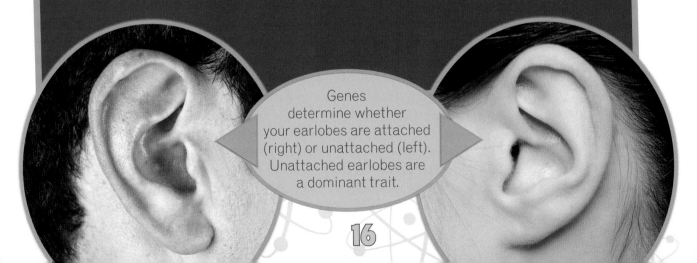

Genes determine whether your earlobes are attached (right) or unattached (left). Unattached earlobes are a dominant trait.

# GRAPHIC ORGANIZER: A PUNNETT SQUARE

**MOTHER**

|  | B | b |
|---|---|---|
| **B** | BB | Bb |
| **b** | Bb | bb |

**FATHER**

A Punnett square shows the different possible outcomes when genes are combined. This Punnett square looks at eye color. This mother and the father both have a gene for brown eyes (B) and a gene for blue eyes (b). Their eyes are brown because that is the dominant gene. There is a one in four chance that their offspring will get two recessive blue-eye genes and have blue eyes (bb).

# What Is DNA?

People, such as Mendel, have been studying heredity for hundreds of years. It was not until recently that scientists had the tools to see what was really going on, though. In the early 1950s, scientists found DNA in the cell's nucleus.

DNA is a tiny **molecule** inside the chromosomes. It holds

DNA is like a blueprint with the plans for building all the parts of the cell.

all the information that makes living things what they are. DNA looks like a twisted ladder. The ladder's rungs are made up of pairs of the four main bases in DNA. These bases are A, C, T, and G. Groups of these bases form the genes, sort of like the way combinations of letters form different words.

Scientists study the DNA of organisms to learn about the genes they form.

# Genetic Disorders

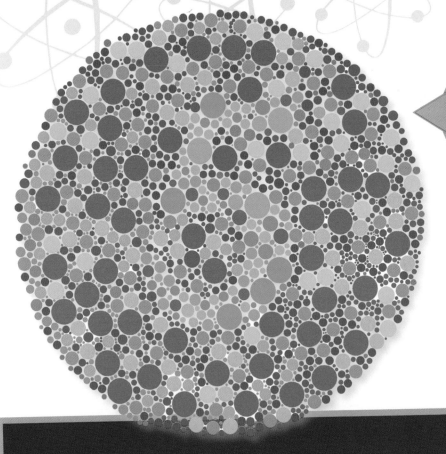

A person who has red-green color blindness has trouble seeing the number five in this picture.

Just as eye color and other traits can be passed on, so can disorders, or illnesses. One common disorder that is passed from parents to offspring is red-green color blindness. A person with this disorder cannot tell the difference between red and green. More serious disorders can be passed on, too.

Cystic fibrosis, which is an illness of the lungs, is a genetic disorder. Sickle-cell anemia, which affects the blood, is, too.

Scientists can test for some disorders. They know which genes cause them and how to look for them. Other disorders are harder to pinpoint. There is a lot more to learn about DNA and our genes.

People with sickle-cell anemia have blood cells that are C-shaped (left) instead of round (right). This can cause the person to have several health problems.

Cystic fibrosis causes difficulty with breathing, lung infections, and other health problems.

# Learning About Ourselves

Scientists are mapping DNA to crack the code of all the different genes it holds. By studying the DNA of different species, scientists can trace the history of a species through its ancestors. They can also track changes in traits over time.

As they learn more about DNA, scientists hope to unlock clues about genetic disorders and maybe even correct them.

Another goal in understanding human DNA is curing illnesses. Many genetic disorders come from **mutations**, or problems in a gene. The hope is that this could fix the mutation, which would then fix that disorder. Imagine all the illnesses that could possibly be cured as scientists continue to learn about heredity!

# GLOSSARY

**cells** (SELZ)  The basic units of living things.

**chromosomes** (KROH-muh-sohmz)  The parts of cells that hold the code that controls the body's features.

**dominant** (DAH-mih-nent)  In charge.

**genes** (JEENZ)  Tiny parts in the centers of cells. Genes tell your cells how your body will look and act.

**heredity** (her-ED-uh-tee)  The passing of features from parents to children.

**molecule** (MAH-lih-kyool)  The smallest bit of matter possible before it can be broken down into its basic parts.

**mutations** (myoo-TAY-shunz)  Changes in genes that can cause problems.

**proteins** (PROH-teenz)  Important elements inside the cells of plants and animals.

**recessive** (rih-SEH-siv)  Having to do with a gene that does not give traits unless there are two present.

**reproduce** (ree-pruh-DOOS)  To make more of something.

**resemble** (rih-ZEM-bul)  To look like.

**species** (SPEE-sheez)  One kind of living thing. All people are one species.

**sperm** (SPERM)  A special male cell that, with a female egg, can make a baby.

**traits** (TRAYTS)  Features that make an individual special.

# INDEX

# WEB SITES

Due to the changing nature of Internet links, PowerKids Press has developed an online list of Web sites related to the subject of this book. This site is updated regularly. Please use this link to access the list:
www.powerkidslinks.com/lels/heredity/